MW00528633

限度

GENDO REIKI

The Art of Self Honor

I dedicated this book in memory of my mother and in honor of my ancestors.

限度

GENDO REIKI

The Art of Self Honor

by: Lisa Okochi

Lime Press

Gendo Reiki: The Art of Self Honor by Lisa Okochi

This book is written to provide information and motivation to readers. It's purpose is not to render any type of psychological, legal, or professional advice of any kind. The content is the sole opinion and expression of the author, and not necessarily that of the publisher.

ISBN: 978-1-953584-80-9 E-book
ISBN: 978-1-953584-81-6 Paperback
ISBN: 978-1-953584-82-3 Hardback
Printed in the United States of America.

Lime Press LLC
425 West Washington Street Suite 4
Suffolk, VA 23434 US
https://www.lime-press.com/

TABLE OF CONTENTS

INTRO:

Change is the healthiest way to survive.
-Karl Lagerfeld

Where we are: For the first time since World War Two, we are experiencing deep fear of the unknown. We see exactly how we personally react and how we are coping...or not, in a 'what if' Stephen King type scenario that is real. How have you been handling things? Did you surprise yourself with resilience or slide into paralytic fear or depression? It's like psychological warfare isn't it; a game to test our management skills on all levels of our lives, to see if we can trust in ourselves that we can pull through and not let fear blind us to the fact that change is good, that change is needed, despite the upheavals. A test of true Faith.

It goes without saying that the biggest weapon of 2020 has been Fear and Separation and the number one highlighted reaction it caused most individuals is **Stress**. I say 'most' because it's obvious that a certain number have gained wealth and happiness by investing in or having the right product or service at the right time and bless them their prosperity as long as they don't abuse their advantage with greed.

I have been quite busy helping clients and groups

cope and lessen anxiety because that is my field; to help people heal and find inner peace. But I must admit, even though I thought I was an introvert and happy to be by myself but honestly? It did get to me during the first half of the year that I was not able to meet anyone. I was teaching on zoom and talking up a storm with each of my friends, and relatives on the phone... but it was immensely lonely at times. It truly taught me how much we humans *need* to be seen and heard physically.

I thought I was calm and dealing well but my hair began to shed alarmingly over summer and I discovered my iron level dropped dangerously low. On the other hand, despite my initial bouts of loneliness, I have been feeling very balanced with great energy and I am sleeping better than I had in years, suffering from insomnia. Yes, I am affected by stress and likely to experience it like any other person but you see, the difference is how I handle it. As you read about my story in this book, I have trained many years in the art of inner stillness which I hope to share with you. Although I have my moments of anxiety like everyone else, I do not let fear in. For there's one thing I have complete control over and that is my emotions. **And so do you**. But as long as you don't address the clutter and build up of your emotional stress, trauma or inertia, the blockages will keep you stuck in a repetitive cycle of a broken record.

Where are you at this point? What's your broken

record about?

If you always seem to be surrounded by drama, it is your responsibility to become aware if you are reacting to the game by knowingly or unknowingly responding in a way that triggers and continues the drama of "he said, she said". You can talk about being the victim, someone being too needy or enabling…it doesn't really matter because what you are missing is awareness and **perception**.

If you are overwhelmed with too much responsibility working long hours, then coming home to cook and clean up for the family alone and maybe also taking care of a sick member, not getting enough sleep or me time…and perhaps complaining to a friend of how stressed out you are… how much of it is really unfair or is it in fact a question of your inability to ask others for help or not creating boundaries to say no?

Whatever type you may fall under or not, the common thread through most stories is you are not being **heard**. **Your voice** is not speaking your real truth of who you are. Have you noticed how you regularly overhear conversations in public, on trains, in restaurants and perhaps 90% are venting or complaining or commiserating in another's drama or gossiping of others? From my perspective, I think that is our way of releasing some of the stress. A need, although negative. For someone to **listen and hear them**.

It is a survival tool and I am by no means immune

to it either. We struggle to get things right and we need a good friend or two to be soundboards. However it perpetuates the emotional blockages and doesn't heal you to complain. According to Canadian Neuropsychologist Donald Hebb, repetitively complaining over the same issues creates a fixed pattern in the brain that's hard to break free from. When the blockages are cleared, you can perceive how stuck you can be and will move forward to free yourself from the chains. Or maybe you **are** aware you are stuck and see this lockdown as an opportunity and even know what you want but don't know where to start nor actually know what you want to change because fear and doubt still override your efforts or willpower.

If there's said to be four main categories that people want to be successful in, in order to feel fulfilled, they are: Relationships, Health, Wealth and Career. But it's in our human nature to tend to want it all with the least amount of effort and as fast.as possible. Even when we see the red flags early on, we tend to ignore possible unfavorable outcomes or consequences because we think things will "change". This is a cause for chaos and imbalance emotionally if you see success as equal to needing aggressive action to keep on top of life. I tend to think this is a major reason why many have experienced extreme anxiety in and since 2020 because we were literally stopped in our tracks when we are programmed to be on-the-go.

If there's one thing we humans need, it's a level of certainty in our society. We want to feel we are in control, secure in the predictability of routines based on a reliable social structure. It's the uncertainty of our current international predicament that is causing major stress although isolation is a primetime opportunity to take a good look at yourself and your life choices. Do you really know yourself and know what you want?

For there is one certainty: If you are looking to change your life, **NO one can do this shift but You**. That's where you do have control. **You** are responsible for your emotions and choices and it's time for your true voice to be heard; not through aggression but through creativity and zen calmness.

Gendo Reiki is all about pulling you out of your fears and anxieties by clearing the emotional, energetic blockages, getting yourself grounded so that you perceive your broken record with an awakened sense of clarity. Attuning to the healing power of Gendo Reiki will give you the momentum needed to change, as it will smoothly guide and encourage you to set up healthy boundaries to make better choices.

I believe we need to stop talking so much and start learning how to be still and **listen**. I want to bring in an ancient eastern mind/heart healing technique to the west to help you see how much simpler it can be for you to adjust to life circumstances without bogging you down with introspective exercises or talk.

Instead, I am offering a new easier way to find balance by re-wiring your energy.

This is reset.

Chapter 1:

How it started

Peole are always telling me how much they love Japan. How lovely and polite they are. Respectful. Continually offering their assistance and wanting to be of service. Everything is super clean and safe. When you go to the train stations, you see workers carefully wiping down the trash cans and changing all the trash bags every morning. The way they methodically yet respectfully wrap a gift, serve tea, arrange flowers. They are a group oriented society, that is ingrained in them from centuries ago. I feel this Zen honor flowing deep in my DNA and I believe the Japanese society is successful because they are coming from their DNA roots. They act from the concept of mindfulness and approach of 'How can I be of service?'.

It's interesting to study how they behaved after the devastating earthquakes in recent years. Towns along the coastlines were destroyed by huge tsunamis. Families displaced. But friends who were there said right after the initial shock and fear, everyone basically just shook off the dust from their hands and immediately set out to rebuild, sharing food supplies etc. There was no looting. No demonstrations. They calmly moved forward. Simultaneously in Tokyo, where I lived over 20 years, another friend told me that this same big earthquake tremor happened near the end of a workday. He said it was almost eerie. People calmly walked out onto the streets heading home the best way they could find. Thousands of people in their dark suits. Trains were down but there was no pushing or shoving at bus stops. Everyone seemed intrinsically aware that order was of importance and that panic delays results. Such stories and observations are simply to help you see how one can live in a Zen way. It is not to say they don't have any cultural issues like any other country.

My maternal grandparents early 1900s

I remember as a little girl whenever I was sick or hurt myself, my Japanese grandmother would come over, say a Japanese mantra over the hurt area and then she'd blow on it three times telling me it's all better now. Growing up, I was in and out of hospital many times and I recall my mother placing her hands over my chest or on my feet and I would feel better not knowing quite what she was doing. She'd tell me she watched my grandmother do it growing up, when someone was sick. I almost died a few times and was told by drs that I'd be on steroid treatment for the rest of my life.

I grew up in the West. I was never really able to communicate with my Japanese parents until we moved back and as my Japanese improved, I started to question them about my ancestors. I discovered that on my maternal side, there were healers. My great grandfather was a Japanese priest in the Meiji era (late 19th century to early 20th). My mother remembers living with him as a little girl, when he'd predict things that came true soon after. I learned that a prominent monk once came to my grandmother when she was young and told her she was meant to heal people. He gave her a sacred Japanese mantra to repeat 3x whenever someone was sick. This was around 1908. My mother clearly remembers some neighbors coming to her mother in deep pain and leaving completely better. As they grew up, my mother and Aunt helped her give healings too but none of them were trained. There was no official name back in the early 1900s but in fact, they were doing energy healing. This was before anyone heard of Usui, founder of traditional Reiki.

My maternal great grandfather seated in front

I was always searching for ways to battle medication. Countless herbal treatments, acupuncture, water therapy, hypnotism....nothing was sustainable... There was a period I wanted to end my life. I was young and missing out on the fun of being a teenager but I soon gave up those dark thoughts when I saw my father and later my younger brother break down in tears when I impulsively told them. And then one day my mother asked me to take a leap and throw all medications away and start from scratch. I remember I didn't hesitate one second. I was filled with intense trust and faith in that moment that I could let go of my fear of ending up hospitalized without my medicine. It was pure hell for weeks detoxing but somehow I pulled through with her support. My immune system was badly scarred from the steroids so from my late teens I began a new journey into meditation, going on retreats to temples, chanting with monks and sitting under freezing waterfalls. I had several powerful mentors that just walked into my life at critical turning points and shared their wisdom and healing knowledge and I felt a strong connection and pull to study the concept of Energy for healing and I practiced Ashtanga yoga for years and got certified in many alternative healing modalities.

And throughout this period I still managed to graduate from a prestigious university in Tokyo in Intercultural Communications. I was and still am, a fighter inside. You see, there was this other side to me that took on each challenge with a certain detached, calmness. It wasn't a disassociation but more of a quiet endurance in suffering, even as a child, like I innately knew that inner stillness was important to overcome obstacles. From this vantage point, I learned how to strategize to get to certain goals without losing emotional control. It wasn't until my mother studied our family tree that I began to realize the significance of how I got to be who I am today.

My family emblem of samurai lineage: 3 butterflies protecting a chrysanthemum

My Paternal lineage

I became more curious and only recently learned that on my paternal side, my lineage originates from Samurai that trace back to the Heian period (700 A.D). I understand that at one time, they used to directly protect the Emperor of Kyoto. I knew my surname (Okochi), was of Samurai origin but I realized the significance of my ancestors and how their warrior power still flows through my DNA as do the healing energies from my maternal side. The two are part of me, creating a practical training to realign internally and retain it without trying too hard and through observation of my students, the results are significant. It's been a long meditative journey of understanding, fine-tuning, and self-discovery, having studied many different modalities in different cultures over three decades. It is time to share it.

Chapter 2:

What is Gendo Reiki: 21st Century Healing

Gendo Reiki (hard "G" sound as in "get"), GR, is a hybrid healing system that has a quicker frequency to pull you out of stagnancy, fear or overwhelm and help you become more self-aware and in control of your life. It is unique because it creates interaction between three separate modalities; utilizing healing power to clear emotional blockages, developing ability to perceive and create stronger boundaries (which has been a trending concept), and to live the Zen Way of honoring yourself.

It doesn't take pain away so much as to help you disperse it by being calm to look at it, to hopefully perceive the core story of your issue. Once you awaken to why a certain pain or emotion is stuck in you after **GR** clearing, then you might find the right way to address it. Take my asthma for instance, for years I assumed it was a medical health issue and that it was just my constitution. However once I delved into healing alternatives and practiced inner stillness, I realized it was coming from a steady buildup of acute resentment towards my mother for not letting me go out to meet friends or go to parties like my brothers because "You will get sick"...and I **would** get sick... This was her constant mantra whenever I planned to go have fun, even after being in my 30's and I had been healthy for a few years! Me, angry? I used to think I was shy and obedient. Then it dawned on me, **yes**! I was furious and blamed her for my illness. Once I allowed myself to see this, I became quite resentful at first, that I missed out on my youth then I started to release it during my training and I began to understand how the game involved two players. I wasn't a victim. It was a powerful lesson on setting boundaries. I was as much a part of the role playing as she was and this is what Gendo Reiki will help you see and perhaps clear for you in order to be free. Oh and by the way, my story does end happily with deep mutual love and respect because we forgave ourselves and each other. She has been my greatest supporter in my life.

> *"Remember :You can't truly function and find harmony in your life if you are not calm inside"*
> *Jessica Figueroa*

What is Gendo?

Gendo is a Japanese term I use to best describe my unique approach to applying Reiki to maximize success in the four categories of life: Health, Love, Career and Wealth and like many Japanese expressions, it carries more than one connotation.

Gendo 限度: Definition: ′(Geh.n.doh), limit: mainly refers to the amount that is allowed mentally and in common sense.′

'**Gendo**' generally means 'limit' but in order for you to understand the nuance of it's meaning, it is useful to know how it contrasts with another Japanese word, '**Genkai,**' which is an extreme form of 'limit'.

Genkai 限界: Definition: (Geh.n. ka.i), limit: refers to the maximum amount that can ensure safety. Exceeding this amount is dangerous.

Both terms can describe several types of common stressful situations many of us easily find ourselves in, no matter our social status or educational background. I am taking the liberty to use these terms to best describe my way of looking at and developing one's boundaries as I find the English term too heavy and set as some people can be locked down and need to break free from too many boundaries. So in my teachings, I like to refer to boundaries as Gendo or Genkai 'lines', using the Japanese nuances to help you see where you may need to redefine yours in order to lead a more fulfilling life where your voice is heard and respected *and* for *you* to be able to discern where others have their lines.

NOTE: Although I will be breaking down GR into

the 3 categories as mentioned above, I want to explain that the type of healing I do can result in the culmination of all 3 and more. Gendo can stand on its own but it will be the reiki that will help you create your limits naturally and heal other components in your life.

What is Gendo: The Five Types

The following describes certain real case personalities types who create their own high stress based on weak or compensated Gendo lines.

Type 1 situation: The Pleaser with vague lines

This is the type that gets stressed out for their inability to say no and end up in constant dilemmas and inner conflict, who tend to complain to others of what they have to do but in reality they do have a choice to be selective.

Case 1: Ellen. She used to always say yes to everyone to please them and maintain harmony even at her own cost. Putting everyone first exhausted and stressed her because she often didn't want to do whatever it was but she feared to upset people. She is a Doctor in one of New York's leading hospitals and for as long as she's worked there, certain staff members dumped their workloads on her and there was one in particular who always pressured her to change her schedule at the last minute. She had only completed part of the Gendo reiki when she told me she really realized she allowed herself to reach her "Genkai"(reaching her limits to let people cross her boundaries) and feeling a sense of her inner Samurai, she finally started to refuse taking on others' responsibilities and realized she had nothing to fear from them. If anything, they respected her more and she's enjoying less stress and more freedom.

People are funny. We want others to be nice to us but if you are too nice, we are likely to exploit that selfishly and it is considered a weakness in our society. Being too nice and accommodating ironically doesn't gain you respect. We can be mean that way... Are you being treated as a 'doormat' or pushed around?

Gendo, means 'outlining or measuring' the amount you'd want for your boundaries. It is very different from **Genkai**,which means having others disrespect and trespass into your personal space to the point you 'had enough"' and want to lash out. Both terms imply your 'limit', however **Gendo** is about **knowing where you draw the line** and **Genkai** is **letting people cross the lines**. In Gendo, you have the control but the latter, you let others take control. Gendo will help you learn what is non-negotiable to you. You need boundaries so people don't take advantage of you and you need them to determine choices you make to be happy.

In other words, if you can't clarify what works for

you to your own self, whether in a relationship or in a job, your choices or decisions will have unstable results.

Here's a simple example of Gendo: Your home is your physical boundary in society. But let's imagine it represents your interaction with others. No one can enter your personal space without your permission. The walls within it are the boundaries of the rooms, the rooms being various aspects of your present life; work, love, family etc. The Gendo boundaries would be who you allow into your home and how far. It's your choice. Would you allow a takeout delivery person to enter your home? If you set your Gendo line at the living room and keep your bedroom door closed, and an acquaintance checks out the bedroom uninvited, how would you feel? What if all visitors kept doing that when you don't like it? You *allowed* them to 'cross the line' until you reached your 'Genkai'. You are emitting some kind of unclear energy that makes them think its ok and they will continue to do so, maybe escalate, because you didn't draw the line. So like your dream home, you'd want it to be on a solid foundation with a clear flow between rooms and open space where you'd want to invite life in or not.

Type 2 situation: The Martyr with barricaded lines

This is the type that takes on everyone's responsibilities and is unappreciated because they don't know how to communicate strongly and they tend to absorb everyone's negative energies. They get bullied and can't stop the verbal abuse. They have low self esteem. It can be brutal if children grow up witnessing this interaction because they are likely to think it's common and can treat people that way growing up.

Case 2: Alice. When she started the Gendo process with me a few years ago, she was in a very stressful situation at work under a severe boss and going through intense family dysfunction with a very abusive, alcoholic husband and belligerent adult son who was copying his father's behavior towards her. She was overwhelmed at work and extremely stressed, sad and lonely at home. She wanted a divorce and thought of quitting work many times but she felt paralyzed and just didn't have the courage. So for years she suffered in this situation. She was very private, not confiding in anyone so she didn't know she was at her **Genkai** limit. She didn't have any Gendo lines but rather built walls that had become thick barriers to make her feel safe. But as she finished the Gendo Reiki, she became stronger. In a short time, she started to stand up for herself and finally pushed her husband out of her life. At work, she stood up against her boss in an honorable way that in the end, gained her boss' respect. Her reputation at work has also increased as did her income and she maintains it using the 3 minute tool of Gendo, which has helped her and her clients.

Many people endure suffering thinking they
are being patient, hoping things will change but in
reality they do not know where their boundaries lie.
Manipulators instinctively pick up on these types
and don't want you to develop your Gendo stance.
Keep in mind this also means other people might
not have boundaries themselves. The shift occurs
when the victim chooses to become the creator and
steps into control. Once you break out and away
from manipulative control, the positive vibrations of
success can find you. The 'Me Too' movement is a
good example. Gendo lines allow for healthy choices
and to be open to change. Now, I am referring to lines
you draw, not walls. Lines that you can expand as you
shift. It's not about building walls to shut out life. But
you will learn to shut out the ones who don't respect
your Gendo lines.

I met Alice the other day (May 2020), to check in
with her. She told me she knows it was the Gendo
Reiki which has transformed her and she says she
has used the 3 minute tool to heal a friend going
through heart surgery last year and the doctors
took notice that he recovered much faster than they
expected. She uses it regularly to keep the harmony
at work and has developed a better relationship with
her formerly abusive son as well.

Her ex will never get near her. She is living the

Samurai way using integrity and creating her self boundaries by honoring herself.

Her life has truly shifted and she told me she loves who she has become because she is able to be more authentic instead of putting up a front. Her internal "hertz" has balanced and is now shifting her to be more physically active and improve her diet. It certainly was good to see how she was smiling so much more and looking focused.

When you come from a zen place, you will become more genuine and allow yourself to be you.

Type 3 situation: The Protector with unprotected lines

This is the type that is so often overlooked because their occupations are in law enforcement, Correction facilities, Frontline, etc. We see them already with powerful boundaries (not lines) to protect society and themselves, however they don't realize they are regularly bombarded with anger, resentment, grief and despair and also exposed to a lot of horrific scenes average people never see except on TV. They have physical walls but no awareness of how they need to protect themselves energetically and release the **emotional** stress **everyday**.

Case 3: Frank. He has been a Correction officer Lieutenant for many years, working in a facility and dealing with very violent inmates and he had become so drained and exhausted that he turned to healing modalities to find ways to cope with the stress. Even on his days off he couldn't shake off the heaviness.

He came to my GR (Gendo Reiki), group with a fellow partner who worked in the most dangerous ward and when they walked in, they looked very heavily stressed, hardly able to even smile. Their eyes looked dull and both looked sluggish like they were just going through the motions. He told me how tough the work environment was, constantly on alert and how they tried traditional reiki and other modalities but didn't get strong results. It was rewarding to see the transformation in both as they became more aligned after each level. Even the other students noticed. They looked refreshed and lighter. Their eyes were clearer like a fog had lifted. He told me it was the first time he actually felt different, alive..compared to the other modalities he tried.

Think of how many who don't know their Gendo limits regarding how much they can handle a stressful situation on their own. They have numbed down their feelings to survive in a work field, including long-term caregivers, all of whom are likely juggling other situations as parents, partners, etc. They are the ones who already are past their Genkai limits but have built such a strong wall of defense to cover it up that they don't know how to climb out of it and are too proud to ask for help. The stress of holding on through sheer will power compromises their health, sleeping and eating habits and their relationships. This is especially true for men who feel like they have to put on a guard to protect their family or for the women who are working in a predominantly male environment and who also might be single mothers. When this type keeps going beyond their **Genkai**, their stress levels can push them out of control or make them disrespect the Gendo boundaries at home, domestic violence being the extreme case. Is the offer of a helpline really something these types would reach out for?...

They need healing too and self-awareness. Gendo Reiki can help clear the numbness and perhaps loosen their guard down enough for them to acknowledge the need to rebalance themselves and learn how to practice emotional protection.

On a follow up of the Correction Officer, he told me he was practicing GR every morning for work to be controllable and he doesn't feel as much of that heaviness as before. He also felt that the ward where he works seems less agitated. You see, when you come from a calm place, your energy subtly shifts the atmosphere so certain people can sense that and stop being as defensive or closed up. He finally added that he believed the Law enforcement needed this GR which was rewarding to hear.

The Gendo stance is to be calm under pressure and to be able to hold one's ground with integrity when you feel someone is not respecting you. Your body and mind can only function well when you are calm inside. To develop a Zen Way of being increases your perception of situations, from a centered state versus an aggressive one.

Even the level of or lack of clutter in your home and office is a form of self honoring your inner boundaries. That is why Marie Kondo, (organiser expert), is so popular. She sees decluttering as an art and a form of zen honor too. Objects have frequencies so you feel less density with minimalism.That's why our minds feel clearer. Decluttering can make one see how many other areas in life you need to "draw the line" to achieve healthy relationships. Gendo is very much like decluttering your mind and life. It isn't about acquiring intellectual knowledge nor is it about psycho-analyzing. It is a practice.

Type 4 situation: The Workaholic with unequal lines

This is also a common type that accumulates stress from over achieving. They will be consumed with a career oriented goal or they compete so aggressively, they forget the need for balance in other areas, often ignoring the signs to slow down or they push relationships aside, convincing themselves that their partner understands and will stand by them even though they are being neglected.

Case 4: Mark. A professional who juggles many hats and was constantly overflowing with projects and deadlines and pushing himself past his realistic limits. He'd cram his brain with to-do lists. He even spoke so fast, he'd trip over his words...Every so often he'd collapse with fatigue for a couple days then get right back on overdrive. After the GR, he says he started to catch himself and slowed down enough to enjoy his success. He admitted he never thought he was 'enough', that he wasn't deserving. He became conscious of habits that just weren't serving him anymore and made time to socialize. He's able to focus on simplifying and maximizing results. It also helped him try out challenges in other artistic fields he'd previously doubted could be possible for him.

The workaholic type will keep adjusting his Gendo lines to let in more work and projects, thereby sacrificing space for relationships and health. He works overtime and still gets up extra early to keep up. He works to up his career at all costs or to prove himself to someone. It's not about how he can be of service to others so much as enjoying or needing to win the game or get recognition, perhaps. But this unequal distribution of Gendo lines can ultimately break apart because it's two dimensional. Healthy lines come from a balance in all aspects of your life.

Type 5 situation: The Robot with canned lines

This is the type who is more or less stuck in a zone like the movie "Groundhog day" with Bill Murray. They have Gendo lines that are set but unproductive. They often won't want to try out new things or go anywhere and don't want to shift their lines. Yet inside, their heart is crying.

Case 5: Seth. A young man who was just going through the motions every day with no specific interest in anything or anyone. He would have what I call a Canned routine where every day has the same set schedule; wake up, eat breakfast, go to work, come home, eat dinner, watch tv and go to bed. He was neither liked nor disliked, and he had no inclination to improve any aspect of his life and yet he yearned for change but unsure of what he wanted to change.

When I first met him for a consultation I recognized his dull heavy energy but at the same time I perceived his hidden intelligence and sensed he was coming near his Genkai. He wanted to shift. This type is unfortunately very common, from students to retirees. They don't have a clear direction so they are unmotivated but still go on, likely isolated and feeling depressed. They really don't seem to know how to honor themselves and they feel safe within canned routines but in reality they are often scared to let go because it's the one thing they are sure will always be there.. routines. This can also happen to people who are grieving. Set routines are their way of coping through loss.

Another reason to emphasize the need to set your healthy Gendo lines is that you otherwise might be unable to see when you or someone are unwittingly pushing into other's like a Gatecrasher. I'm sure you know these types. They are the ones who don't know to respect one's time or know when to end a conversation even if you are looking at your watch or trying to get ready to leave...who might simply assume that a professional 'line' can become a 'friend' one with no ill intent. The other person might blame it on insensitivity, bad manners or selfishness when it actually was more about learning where social lines are. GR will help you hone your perception to pick up on the signs and lead you to develop more social skills.

What is Reiki?
霊気 (ray.key)

Reiki, is becoming known as a healing modality in the west. "Rei- 霊" means spirit and "ki-気" means energy. The Chinese character for "ki" is the same for Tai Chi and Qi gong. "Ki","Chi" and "Qi" simply means energy.

Traditional Reiki is a healing technique where the practitioner clears energetic blockages in the mind, body and spirit. This is an example of what is termed as 'Energywork' which will be explained in the next chapter. Reiki basically teaches that our bodies have 7 main energy centers that each govern certain organs and emotions. These centers are called Chakras which means 'spinning wheels'. These Chakras communicate energetically with each other and can become imbalanced when one or more become blocked which hampers the flow of healthy energy much like a river getting clogged with debris. Stressful events or pent up emotions are the main causes of blockages. They believe that if you accumulate too much stress, lets say frustration, then it will manifest in a tightness in your stomach and if you continue to be aggravated, you start to get digestive issues. Or if you build up stress from work overload, the Chakra center in your head gets blocked, leading to headaches. You get the gist.

Reiki practitioners are trained to 'feel' or sense the energy health of Chakras with their hands without touching, and are able to clear them. Sacred symbols are used to enhance the healing and clients usually feel very relaxed. It is an art form that acknowledges the **spirit inside us**, which modern medicine does not address. That is the issue in western society. We are not just a physical mass of bones, organs and muscles nor are we mainly the mind. We are body, mind and spirit and we need holistic attention. I feel our society separates them completely, overmedicating or talking through things too long which are often just bandaging people who are really more in need of energetic clearing and aligning. When one of my friends was interning at a major hospital in New York, he told me they are taught to just prescribe the highest dosage and hope for the best and that it's fairly impossible to keep up with the new medicines and the difference between similar ones and side effects. How sad is that. The fact is, it is hard to function in any way if you are not calm inside and stress or anxiety is usually why you are not. Stress is the major source of many illnesses. Reiki is one easy way to start the process of calming down holistically. There is a need to start preventing illness by learning inner calmness.

Most people wonder how it can possibly work. But the evidence is clear in many accredited clinical trials and experiences that it helps improve well being.

So what is Gendo Reiki?

> *"If an egg is broken by an outside force, life ends. If broken from the inside, life begins. All great things begin on the inside." Devin Weafer*

Combining "Gendo" and "Reiki," like any creation, I discovered a new variation of Reiki through my own ancestral background and training. There is more of an earth grounding quality to it that brings out the kind of warrior we all have in us. The part of you that knows 'enough is enough' comes to the surface.

Gendo Reiki is a powerful therapeutic process that

works to release the emotional and mental constraints that we often carry around, year after year, preventing us from knowing where our boundaries are. Free from this dead weight, less stress, clear vision and decisive action are more easily realized.

It is adapted for groups as well as individuals and it is a different direction than psycho-analyzing the causes behind the stress, past or present. To practice Gendo Reiki is to have a different relationship with yourself - I mean that you will still have the memories and perhaps scars of your past but you can develop a different perspective of those experiences, and insights that may help you put closure on them.

"Never be a prisoner of your past. It was just a story, not a life sentence" Anonymous

Take one of mine for example. One of the side effects from medication is that I lost the sight in one eye. At 20, my self-esteem was deeply damaged for years. I pushed away several possible relationships. But this Reiki has enabled me to see how it helps me empathize in my work. Yes, it's there but I no longer focus on it or blame it. I choose to see it as making me stronger nowadays and I no longer feel a victim. Gendo Reiki can thus change your thoughts about something which will change how you feel about it. Healing your stress with reiki and developing Gendo complement each other to form stable results.

There are no sacred symbols or rituals in Gendo Reiki. It's different from a healing session because it is more of an attunement (I will explain this in the next chapter). This variation has a grounding energy which seems to naturally shift and motivate clients to make changes in their lives that create balance and more self confidence. It can move the energy of your thoughts to manifest past your doubts and fears. It also gives you the ability to help others feel calmer or less anxious using a 3-minute tool.

So if your stress is due to being in a bad relationship or having to work at a job you hate, you will develop clarity after the Gendo process that may make you see your need to set better Gendo lines of what you will tolerate in a relationship or finally decide to switch to a more meaningful career.

Let me share with you how a recent client has shifted. Jenny initially came to me to help her through the grief of losing her best friend during Covid. She was in deep mourning and getting no sympathy from her partner. She let work slide and she said she couldn't function for the last 3 months. GR not only clears but it also energizes and wakes up your energetic system. Within just a month not only has she released most of her grief, she truly saw how stuck she was in her relationship with a man who disrespected and verbally put her down for years. She also became painfully aware of how very cluttered her whole house was. She knew of all the issues in her life for *years* but never had the motivation to do anything about it all. As she went through the attunements, I coached her into riding on the waves of them to shift her life. I did not suggest to her to break up which would be the popular response. But we worked on her *perspective.* For the first time, she stopped reacting to her husband's verbal abuse and yelling by calmly stopping him each time, telling him she won't tolerate it. He expected her to yell back like she's been doing for 12 years and he's realizing he can't trigger her anymore. It's tough for her at times but her shift is noticed and he is not yelling as much. The biggest surprise for her is that she finally started a major decluttering of her home! Even her husband voluntarily pitched in. She can't believe it herself except she knows it's from the GR and since the other benefit of it is she can heal others too with the 3-minute tool, she has been able to also calm down her child *and* the babies in her daycare center. This is such a marvelous and rewarding feeling for both of us and I'm proud of her progress.

This is what we need to define in other aspects of our lives, to honor ourselves. Developing Gendo lines in Health, Love, Career and Wealth. Let's say you were overeating from stress. Once the Reiki healing calms down the stress levels, you regain the natural desire to eat within healthy limits which in turn will give you more self confidence. When stress is lowered, you might realize how controlling you were with your teenage child, for example, so you learn to step back by redefining the Gendo lines between you. It can have you re-evaluate how you want to manage your work responsibilities, etc. You see, Gendo is a Way. The Reiki flows through you to clear your path and Gendo stays with you to rebuild your life. And through observations in myself and my students, I feel many others will benefit.

CHAPTER 3:

SOME BASIC TERMS AND CONCEPTS OF ENERGY

"If you want to find the secrets of the universe, think in terms of energy, frequency and vibration".
– Nikola Tesla

Acupuncturists will refer to energy centers in our body as meridians, which are energetic pathways along which there are acupuncture points to put needles in to unblock stuck energies they are trained to find. Very simply put, a meridian represents an organ and governs emotions much like Chakras. Dis-ease is found along meridians and checking pulses, the state of your tongue and nails. (Trigger points in massage therapy are often right on an acupuncture point.) Qi Gong refers to energy centers such as the Bahui point on the top of your head where the spirit energy comes through and the Tan dien under your naval which is considered the storage tank of life force energy. Reflexology is an ancient technique that sees the feet, hands and ears as having zones correlating to organs as well. These modalities are to name a few of the alternative ways to release stress and what they have in common is the concept of calming down internally to regain well-being. This is Energywork.

Vibration, Frequencies, Hertz, etc.

There are several components moving and being created as you experience the Gendo Reiki (**GR**) process. It is important that you understand that vibration, frequencies, hertz, electromagnetic fields, are interchangeable terms for energy and everything in and around you is moving constantly. You can sit very still, for example, but inside, there's the beat and rhythm of all your organs moving. Inside your head are all those thoughts racing around in your mind. Then there's the energy coming through sounds around you, cars, devices, other people etc., and only to a certain degree, can we manage them through selective hearing or tuning out.

> *"The highest form of ignorance is when you reject something you don't know anything about".*
> *– Wayne Dyer*

One of the main factors that create stress is our inability to control and manage all these Energy signals that are constantly shifting and bombarding us all day long. Science is now able to prove that even our thoughts, emotions and images have a vibration that is not contained in the brain but emit outwards in its own field of energy. It is said that the speed of your thoughts is comparable to the speed of light and sound. It's important for you to understand that this means part of the stress you feel could likely be coming from absorbing the negative thoughts and emotional energies of others.

People can also take from your energy. Have you ever heard of a psychic vampire? Haven't you often had the experience of feeling drained after a friend vents or complains on and on to you and afterwards they tell you they feel so much better? You didn't do anything except listen yet afterwards you are exhausted. Some people unknowingly feed off of people with good energy, leaving the other person feeling depleted without quite knowing why. In the laws of energy, the stronger 'vibe' will magnify and take and absorb from the weaker one. The best way to protect yourself from negative people and situations you find yourself in, is to maintain a strong vibrational energy in yourself. Sounds like science fiction doesn't it? But it's what goes on around you all the time. Of course it goes both ways like when you go to a concert. Initially you might be in a glum mood but then you start getting affected by the excited energy of the crowd and soon become one of them, shouting and whooping with joy. Actually one of the positive sides to isolation is that it keeps you from being affected by other people... your vibration can be at its clearest, as long as you yourself have been in a zen place of peace.

LAW of ATTRACTION

Did you know that it takes **33** milliseconds to pick up a facial expression and **5** seconds to act on an impulse before we pull the brakes? I'm sure you have plenty of instances where you've missed the facial hints and ended up losing an opportunity to impress or net a business deal.. And the times you had a great opportunity to have fun or pursue a challenge but fear got in the way. Practicing GR can push past the fear and act on an impulse that you instinctively feel is good.

Based on this fact that your thoughts and emotions send out energy, those who are skilled at 'reading' people may unknowingly be tapping into the frequency of their moods, thoughts and overall personal vibrations. You can develop this too, and learn to hone your intuitive abilities. I know from my experience, Gendo has heightened my ability to read people and situations faster. It's useful because now I pause and choose words more carefully if I sense misunderstandings. I also used to be quite indecisive because in fact, I wasn't sure of what I wanted - my Gendo boundaries were unclear. But nowadays I don't second guess myself as often and I act with more confidence than before.

Auras, Chakras, thought forms

Why is it that a lot of people shy away from terms such as auras or be skeptical about the chakra system? These same people who think it's all "woo woo" talk have all kinds of slang terms they use that are actually referring to these very same concepts. They are the very ones who would say "Hey you know Steve? I really like to hang out with him. He's got good vibes" or "I don't know about that place.. it gives me the creeps" or what about "let's hire her, I have a good feeling about her"... Who hasn't said things like these countless times? Did you realize that vibes is short for 'vibrations'?

Science is now saying humans and nature, from plants to insects, all emit energy they term "electromagnetic fields" which spiritual teachings have called "auras" for centuries. Auras constantly shift depending on the health or mood of a person. Science now can measure or scan your aura to see how strong your electromagnetic fields is.

You can maintain a healthy vibrant aura wth excercise, love, laughter and just being in an overall good mood. People can feel it. When your friend is gloomy moody, it brings you down too. We affect those around us with our auras.

Now chakras were briefly discussed in the Reiki section and they are energy centers that determine the vibrancy of your aura.There are 7 main chakras as you can see in the image and each one is symbolized by color, emotion and organ.

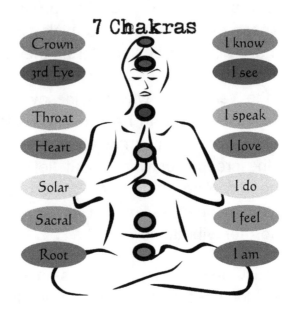

Emotional blockages can accumulate in a chakra and interfere with the energy flow in your body. Most people are not aware how damaging it is to hold on to pent up feelings. GR can address this and help you regain a strong aura again. You will feel more alive and motivated to move forward in life.

Alignment

Ego says "Once everything falls into place I'll find peace". Spirit says "Find your peace and everything will fall into place."

One major term to clarify is 'alignment'. We already understand that any prototype is tested to look for complete alignment of all it's functions before it is put out on the market. Here, we are talking about aligning first internally in our bodies and then externally in our lives. Gendo Reiki focuses on first clearing and energizing your Chakra centers then it clears your perception of external stress factors. Unlike traditional Reiki, scanning or feeling for blockages are not necessary because it's an attunement. Chinese medicine compares the frequencies in our body to an orchestra where each organ and system (nervous system, auto immune system etc), is an instrument. If there's even one instrument that's out of tune or not on the beat, the whole orchestra is out of sync.

Attunement

Much like an instrument that goes off key like guitars or pianos, a tuner would check out each string or key, carefully plucking all the strings or notes as he listens for harmony. You don't just fix one note.

Attuning a body is like that. The practioner is the tuning fork, trained in finding the balance and harmony for you. deeper than a healing session because it stays in you and you can attune others too by passing it on whereas healings cannot be passed on. How? It is like a battery charger I suppose. A healing is a battery that will last only so long but a battery charger can keep it going. The best way to understand this is to experience it.

Stress and Alignment Imbalances

Stress is what usually causes alignment imbalances and that often originates from emotional triggers and feelings. We essentially react and judge from an emotional state and when we hold on to negative feelings, it leads to stress then physical tension. The vibration of stress factors can start going deeper to cause headaches, insomnia etc., and begin to affect the immune system which governs our internal frequencies. Stress is accountable for a majority of illnesses in society.

*"If you do not make time for your wellness, you will
be forced to make time for your illness"*

We need to develop more emotional awareness to
control our stress levels and regularly maintain it with
the least amount of effort. You do not want to wait
until you burn out. When you are emotionally aware,
you can start to protect yourself from other people's
negative energy by maintaining the alignment. Once
aligned, we have to continue tuning ourselves to stay
on top. If you get a new car, it'll become a wreck
if you don't take care of it. Since you don't get to
exchange your body when it breaks down, you have
to periodically dismantle yourself from the inside and
clean up blockages and refuel areas with life force
energy that is a deeper source than breathing.

Internal Realignment

Now let's define what happens as a result of internal
realignment. Your immune system calms the mental
state to be more observant of yourself and your
behavioral patterns. Opportunity arises to redirect
your perception of yourself and your lifestyle, including
attitudes, habits and abilities. Self awareness brings
out the inner wisdom in you that knows how to keep
you balanced and organize your thoughts in the right
direction. You will start catching yourself when you
go off course or revert to old behaviors. You begin to
understand how energy flows between people and
how you too can absorb the moods of others, good

and bad.

Bringing it Together

Gendo helps you to develop a shield against absorbing lower energies that cause imbalances described above. This is a good opportunity for me to explain another aspect of vibrational frequencies that is often discussed amongst energy workers that I think it's time for you to be made aware of; whether you believe it or not is your choice. Anger and fear emit very deep low, static energy that can really affect your well being. The problem is that if you are the target of someone's constant anger or fear, it can absorb into you mentally and physically drain you over time. For example, law enforcement working in narcotics or homicide. Think of all the fear, resentment and anger aimed at them day after day. Law enforcers instinctively develop a certain level of hardness to survive emotionally. The body/mind/ spirit vibration tries to maintain balance and naturally builds a kind of vibrational shield to protect itself in hostile environments. But still the density of negative energies can accumulate in a person to a point of exhaustion. They can carry around a heavy cloud of static frequencies they have absorbed over time and if they don't learn to clear their own frequencies everyday, it leads to burnout, depression, etc. In other words, the exhaustion we sometimes just blame on tight schedules can quite likely be from the energy we absorb off people or people absorbed off of you. Reminder: Energy is never still. It interacts and the stronger vibration (good and bad), tends to absorb the weaker frequency.

This is about a chance to reinvent yourself and create a new Way of being that helps keep out drama and conflicts. A combination of an accelerated form of ancient healing energy that leads you into the Samurai way of Gendo, the art of self-honor and authenticity to succeed. It is a vaccination of life force energy to realign and protect you against the stress, fear and negativity of other people and situations. To establish strong self- boundaries as a natural result because we need the Gendo lines to have structure in life.

> *"Progress is impossible without change, and those who cannot change their minds cannot change anything" George Bernard Shaw*

Chapter 4:

Taking Control of Your Own Health

"If you are going to ask yourself life-changing questions, be sure to do something with the answers".
–Bo Benett

Here's the thing: There are many alternative therapies and beneficial techniques out there and I have tried more than a few and got certified in many but almost all results are temporary and dependent on therapists. It usually involves too much effort, time or money to keep up and maintain. It is not transformational.

If you are reading this, perhaps you are still searching for more self-sustainable ways to stay balanced. If therapy is not really enough, we must change the techniques. And in my experience people don't want an academic program they just want to be less stressed and more focused.

Advantages of Gendo Reiki

There's a very significant edge that GR has over most alternative techniques, especially as society is turning a chapter into a new mindful way of living. The number one reason I enjoy this method is it's versatility. You can adapt it to any strong principles, belief system and customs without needing to replace any other practices you engage in. If anything, GR actually helps make things easier to achieve. It can be used to give you more focus and insight when you are studying or give you more energy to finish a project. It is a non-touch modality that can be done remotely and for groups. Remotely means the practitioner can still align you while based in another location. This is because energy is not confined in space, or time really... Haven't you ever thought how you can talk "real time" with someone who lives in a country that's a few hours ahead? Or wonder how the person you are FaceTiming with is 6 hours behind? I have aligned clients individually or in small groups in Japan, Canada, Switzerland and within the United States such as Texas, Iowa and within my city, New York. Of course one could also experience it in person but all that's needed is a quiet space and a chair. It can't get much simpler than that! And as mentioned earlier, there are no sacred symbols or rituals involved. The practitioner does not need to walk around a client to feel for blockages like traditional Reiki. I highly respect Traditional Reiki and have been certified.

It's absolutely remedial. However, like any traditional style, modern variations and more effective methods are created to match the growth of the advanced world.

We have already briefly discussed such scientific terminology for what Gendo Reiki does: It re-aligns your frequency to the vibrational Hertz of health and well-being to extend and strengthen your electromagnetic field, which is the fundamental source that determines your level of attracting success. Your electromagnetic field is the sum total vibration of your internal energy, your thoughts, your mood, your vitality, etc., emitting outwards to affect how others perceive you and behave towards you and how you behave and perceive situations. So you will be more likely to attract better opportunities when you are in a positive state of being.

GR accelerates growth and self development to help you shift. It surpasses knowledge because it reconnects to a deeper level with the actual systems of the body. This is not so much a program as it *is a process*.

Benefits of Gendo Reiki

The benefits of Gendo Reiki is like a maintenance fuse box with the basic switches you'd need to lead a balanced, successful life, preventing ill health and repelling negative interference. The following are based on results from the many clients I've worked with.

Reduces stress under pressure

Reduces anxiety which prevents panic

Declutters mind

Clears emotional blockages

Relief from persistent emotional pain

Decreases tension within yourself and in relationships

Relief from professional burnout/PTSD

Monitors your thoughts so you **don't react but *respond*.**

Non violent communication

Develops your self-boundaries

Improves strategic/creative thinking

Enhances awareness and appreciation

Have more energy to take action

Creates inner stillness

Acquire the ability to heal others to be calm, including pets

This might appear to be overachieving but really, it's not. They are all connected to the barometer of Stress. It is about monitoring it and learning to pay attention to what triggers stress for you so that you can take preventative measures to lessen it. So therein lies the crux of today's society: People try to cover stress up with medication or they let it accumulate until they develop chronic health issues.

GR is a pioneer practice that even children can master. It's all about aligning your body's Hertz. And it's simple. If it's not simple, it's not sustainable. To achieve and maintain peak levels of success in your career, health, love and wealth, it requires a steady balance of mind, body and spirit. There's no arguing that.

We need to manage stress under pressure

We need to release negative emotions to be open to perceive what we want

We need a balanced state of health

We need to be grounded

We need boundaries to determine our choices and reduce distractions

We want empowerment to feel safe to be yourself

We need to learn the art of samurai detachment

> *"Detachment doesn't mean not caring. It's taking care of yourself first and letting others take responsibility for their actions without trying to save or punish them". Anonymous*

Do you want deeper therapeutic results to help you clean up your lifestyle?

> *"Yesterday I was clever so I wanted to change the world. Today I am wise, so I'm changing myself"*
> *Jalaluddin Mevlana Rumi*

Do you want to be able to take action to manifest your visions?

Chapter 5:

The Gendo Reiki Connection

Have you ever heard of spontaneous synchronization? Some of you may know the example of the pendulum clock shop: If you placed several different clocks ticking at different paces in the same room, after a while all the clocks will be ticking in sync. This was noticed in 1665 by Dutch physicist Christian Huygens. The same happens with metronomes. (Harvard Natural Science).

There's also the experiment of two untuned guitars in the same room where one guitar gets tuned and after a certain time frame the other guitar in the room becomes attuned as well. There are many examples of this type of energetic synchronization.

Similar to this then, Gendo Reiki is a short, accelerated process of getting tuned using higher Hertz of energy. A trained practitioner acts as the facilitator who attunes you. This is a permanent bio-chemical energy exchange. It does not require touch, and would appear as two people simply meditating together. Once this exchange occurs, you can then maintain self-attunements on your own, using the 3-Minute Tool, which I cover in the next chapter.

Similar to streamlining, it is not to be confused with healing, which is temporary and more dependent on the practitioner. A healing is not as deep as an attunement. Attunements plant seeds of transformation that grow at the speed at which you *maintain* and *practice* the Gendo way.

Healings can be very powerful of course but oftentimes the effects wear off because the client may not have guidelines to maintain the healing. They often return home to the same negative thoughts and situations that dissipate the healing effects. However, the Gendo practice is self sustainable and the energy is retrievable at any time if there's a period you lapse, simply by starting up again with your 3-Minute Tool.

The Four Levels of Gendo Reiki

There are 4 levels to the workshops I teach, each with two to three stages, comprising a total of 9 hours. There will be 9 Attunements in total. Each stage will include a 10 minute explanation on how your vibration will shift to higher frequencies of balance, followed by a guided, non-verbal 30 minute attunement. The remaining time is spent practicing the 3-minute tool.

You don't need lengthy lectures to understand it. For

example, to get Wifi, no one cares how that works.. we just want to connect to one, so here, the device is you, connecting to a WiFi service. There are no sacred symbols or academic requirements to master this, except an open mind and desire to improve your quality of health and lifestyle.

As mentioned earlier, if someone were to look in on a typical session, it would appear we were meditating, as we sit in silence in preferably semi darkness. But it is not the same approach as traditional meditation. Traditional meditation tends to be an inward journey of self exploration and understanding. It involves more mental concentration that can be difficult for some students to maintain, especially if you are in a very stressed state or have ADD or severe depression.

Gendo Reiki is outward looking. As the practitioner is balancing out the internal frequencies of clients, level by level, the clients simply sit or lie down and allow themselves to be open to receive the experience of becoming re-aligned. It is relaxing. You are being connected and charged to higher wavelengths. Typical reactions after a session is feeling lighter, having heightened awareness, sometimes initial tiredness, which is a sign of detoxing emotional stress. Between each session, clients practice a 3 minute Gendo Reiki tool to start working on creating better relationships and experiences in the four areas of career, love, health and wealth. It is *not* an analytical process. I'd say it's more of an awareness process.

As a natural course of becoming internally balanced, your perceptions will shift. You will start honing the Gendo way of being authentic, honest and grounded. With clearer boundaries, you have insight to make better choices in your attitudes or approaches. You may notice a sensitivity to places you walk into or people you talk to. The practice becomes a skill based on opening up to the world and engaging the limitless possibilities around us. It becomes a way; an internal source you can tap back into many times, every day. It is accessible and attainable to people in all walks of life.

This is precisely suitable for overwhelmed and stressed people because there's no effort involved during the sessions except to be there and be open to the experience of shifting. You do not need to concentrate with your mind during the process. In fact, like the *Taoist way; don't try too hard or think too hard to get it right.*

I remember when I was in training for a particular healing modality there was this one guy who had high aspirations to share it to his church congregation. He was so enthusiastic he told the teacher he didn't see the point in the first 6 levels of certification. He looked at the results of the last one in the course and wanted to simply learn and teach the last level. It would be like a novice informing a novice how to climb Mt

Everest and then both of them going by themselves. You can imagine the split second disbelief I caught on the teacher's face!

Level One: The Purpose Is To Align
Steps 1-3

The alignment or attunement gradually clears the static and blockages inside your physical, mental and emotional body to prepare you to receive higher vibrations. If you want to understand from a spiritual approach, this level is clearing your Chakras. It's like preparing a fresh cup of coffee. You wouldn't want to pour it over stale, leftover coffee. So you wash the cup to make sure there are no sticky residues. The effects are to clear and re-ground you in your physical body.

Most importantly, this level reconnects you to the energy of the earth. Are you aware of the vibrations of the earth? They call it the Schumann's resonance. In 1952 Dr. Winfried Schumann mathematically predicted that earth behaved like a gigantic electrical circuit. And that it's electromagnetic field surrounds and protects all living things at the natural frequency average of 7.83 Hertz. There is more evidence now that when we aren't in sync with the earth's frequency, we can develop imbalances like anxiety, headaches, immune system disorders,..etc. Have you ever thought how living on this planet's vibration is affecting *you*? To be grounded is to be connected and in sync with the natural flow of life.

Level Two: Achieving Calmness
Steps 4-5

Level Two is about aligning yourself to the hertz of peace and calmness by attuning to the reiki energy of the golden Sun. As the first level grounds you to earth, this level starts to open yourself to higher and lighter vibrations of Peace. The electromagnetic energy of the heart opens up more to life. The brainwaves get activated. It is also said that when the brain waves are in the theta state of inner stillness, it's frequency is at the state of the earth's when it's calm too. Apparently we have the ability to heal ourselves and increase our vitality (life force), when we match the hertz of 7.83, which is the hertz of Earth. (Eric Thompson, Subtle Energy Sciences)

> *"The heart is more powerful than the brain*
> *The heart is about 100,000 times stronger*
> *electrically and up to 5000 times stronger*
> *magnetically than the brain"*
> *Institute of heart health research center*

As I mentioned earlier, the internal alignment needs to happen because it allows you to be able to step back and notice psychological aspects of yourself that influence your attitudes and behavioral patterns. You may realize how closed off your heart has been. The serenity this stage brings you will help you lessen anxiety and give you chances to figure out how to manage issues from a calm state which is highly beneficial in an aggressive, competitive society such as America. We need to start learning that you cannot achieve harmony or balance in yourself nor attract success if you are not calm inside. It also brings awareness to be of service to help others instead of focusing on your own profits.

> *"The ability to observe without judgement is the highest form of intelligence"* Peacelovevibes

Level Three: Bringing in the power of Planets and Pyramids.
Step 6-7

Level Three is attuning to the qualities of planets and the energy of pyramids. We could all use extra help to get to where we want to in life. Just as we all know the sun emits rays to earth and the moon affects the tides, every planet has energetic qualities that help enhance aspects in our lives according to astrology. For example, Mercury governs our ability to communicate and Mars governs how we assert ourselves. The attunements will help you tap into these aspects of planets to further align you.

Here are the major planets and what energetic qualities they represent that you could tap into to help you develop empowerment.

Sun: Is about your Self and your Ego. To stand in confidence. Your social personality

Moon: Is about how you process your emotions and feelings.

Mercury: Is about communication and your ability to speak, explain clearly and be understood.

Venus: Is all about appreciating Love and the Beauty in life and opening up to relationships.

Mars: Is how assertive you are. Courage and willpower.

Jupiter: Teaches you to grab opportunities, have hope and optimism in life. Look for the thrills and challenges.

Saturn: Helps you commit and organize and finish tasks. It is about self discipline.

Uranus: The game changer who loves to throw you off kilter with changes to bring out more individuality.

Neptune: Is focused on your spiritual awareness instead of your Ego.

Pluto: Has the function to empower you to find your destiny in this lifetime. A purpose.

After the planetary attunement you can call upon the qualities of the planet you need. So if you tend to procrastinate or are unmotivated, for example, you could focus on Saturn by using the flow of reiki to connect to it's qualities.

Yogis and meditators have long known of the power

in pyramids and how energy seems to feel higher inside of even a handmade frame of one. Pyramid power will be about creating a crystal grid pyramid through the third eye. This attunement will help deepen your transformation.

Level Four: Forging a Lasting Foundation. Steps 8-9

It is about bringing in all the levels and reinforcing your foundation to create a solid base for you to rebuild on. It anchors you in. This vibrational state can push you to action. There are more people today that have no desires, motivation or intentions to change. There are those too, who have a desire to be motivated and to change but somehow stay stuck. Action and effort **must** happen first to create the motivation to change or find your courage, or passion. It is essential. What I notice is that as you complete this Gendo Reiki process, the natural urge to take action comes out. The instinct awakens to push you toward actually starting that project, join that sports club, call that person etc. You must ride on this momentum and soon it will become a practice.

I have yet to come across a client who didn't experience anything whatsoever.. Mind you, don't assume your experience will be the same as anyone else's. Each one comes in with different levels of imbalance. Sometimes a client initially thinks nothing happened, but close family and friends almost always notice "something's different". When your energy is cleared, you appear calmer and clearer to others.

I will point out one thing though. Some clients who just do the first or maybe up to the second level do not have the same solid results as the ones who complete all levels. Each level has 3 stages of Attunements that initially clears the 'static' of your inner hertz, balances it out then strengthens your total electromagnetic field in a safe, efficient process. For maximum results, you should finish all 4 levels within one time period. You can lose the momentum if you leave too much time between levels and skipping any levels will not be as effective.

Chapter 6 :

Using Gendo Reiki in Your Daily Life

If you were Going to ask yourself life-changing questions, be sure to do something with the answers.
-Bo Benett

The 3 minute Tool: The Art of Manifesting

Did you know science discovered that the electromagnetic field of a healthy heart is 60x stronger than brainwaves? Especially if you add the vibration of Gratitude to it. The Gendo process magnifies the potential of these two forces and we tap into them and apply their vibrations when we use the 3 minute tool.

From the moment you finish the first step in Level 1, the practice begins with the 3 minute technique. It will always be the same technique but it can be applied to so many aspects in your life and it increases in power the further along the process you go and the more you practice. *Take note that the easiest part are the alignments. To maintain it, like anything, you must manage it with regular practice.*

1: First sit with your back straight, feel your feet grounded to the earth. Close your eyes and let them softly focus on the point between your eyebrows. Connect the tip of your tongue to the roof of your mouth and think of an intention. Keep it simple. Take a few slow breaths, breathing the earth energy up through the feet.

2: Next start taking a few deep breaths and tap into the energy of your heart center. Imagine your heart vibration getting stronger and stronger with each breath expanding outwards.

3: Then breathe into your brain, visualizing the brain waves getting stronger and stronger and expanding outwards.

4: Now visualize the intention in the palm of your hands or you could write the word with your finger on the other palm and put your hands into prayer pose at chest level. For example, you have a headache. Visualize a mini you in your hands or write "my headache".

5: See yourself connect to the' "Wi-Fi' frequency of Reiki and say "Reiki please + intention". Ex."Reiki, please dissolve my headache". If you completed level one and two you can say "Gold reiki"

6: Then just remain calm for about 3 minutes and allow the golden sun light of Reiki energy to flow down through your brain, down through your heart, down the arms and into your hands, empowering the intention in them.

7: Feel or visualize the outcome with gratitude then release the intention as you release your hands. The Reiki energy continues to flow to it for about another half hour, so trust in the process.

**Don't think too hard. Instead let your heart and brain energies join into the Reiki and see it magnifying the outcome you desire.

When you set an intention, choose positive words that express the outcome.

Other stress factors to apply Reiki.

Here are some more common things to apply this to, and follow the same steps. It is useful to try to feel the result you want to help the flow.

: When you are tired, visualize the word "energy" with a mini you in your hands and say " Energy. Reiki!". Allow the Reiki to flow and imagine your body becoming awake. Finish with the same instructions as above.

: When you are anxious, do the same technique,

say "Send me peace, Gold reiki"

Feel it disperse the anxiety.

: Angry? Then say " Please calm me down. Reiki!"

When you are really just overwhelmed, unsure etc, you can also simply do the Samurai mudra for 3 minutes and release in the same way at the end.

The Samurai Mudra:

Samurai Mudra

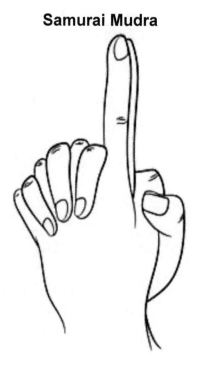

1: Place your hands in a prayer pose and then interlace the fingers and thumbs except for the index fingers pointing up. This is a hand position in yoga called "Kali mudra". It releases old energy and has a strong focused effect and regrounds you. It fits perfectly with the Samurai way of being so I call it the Samurai mudra. I have been teaching this mudra in yoga for several years to energize the class.

2: Take a few slow deep breaths in this mudra, connect to your heart and brain and visualize yourselves grounded and focused as you firmly state "Gendo!" On your next exhale, unclasp your hands and swing your arms downwards and out to the sides. I like to exhale out with the martial art shout "Eiy!" as I sweep hands apart. It feels like a sword cut and cleares the fog away.

**Remember you can do this as often as you want and the more you practice, the more you will feel the Reiki and the more results you'll see and shorter time it'll take. Again: Don't think too hard!

As you complete the higher levels and you begin to notice the shifts happening within you, the clarity Reiki gives you may change the way you perceive yourself. So you can start applying the 3 minute tool adding on the image of reiki being a golden sun ray shining down and flowing through you and use it for: "Peace", "Healing", "wisdom" etc.

If you are going through relationship issues, imagine the person and you in your hands and ask for the Reiki to bring "Peace", "Resolution" etc, and visualize yourselves surrounded in golden sun rays.

There is no wrong way. It's more to do with the vibration of your intention being strong. It's ok to adjust or have your own wording. Just remember to say Reiki to make sure you connected.

Regard this Gendo technique like manifesting with the laws of Attracting being fine-tuned. The edge that you have is that you can apply the energy of Gendo reiki to flow to your intentions instead of just writing or affirming.

Applying the 3 minute tool to help another person or pet

As you complete each level and get accustomed to the 3 minute practice, you may want to try using it when someone close to you, or even your pet, is stressed or ill. It's the same technique except you write the name or visualize the person or both in your hands.

They are the same steps except you are directing the Reiki towards that person. If they are very ill, you can repeat it as often as needed but don't expect to cure them. This is especially effective to calm anxiety in others and remember, calming down helps the immune system repair itself. Doing this with compassion from your heart really is empowering to help in this way. I have worked with pets using Gendo reiki too and owners have noticed the difference.

Disconnecting after giving a healing

<u>Remember</u>: when you send your thoughts or intentions to heal someone else, be it a friend or pet, your vibrational frequency will interact with theirs. It may take a few tries for you or them to notice any changes, **but do practice disconnecting the exchange afterwards** simply by using your hand in a slicing motion in front of your heart to cut the connection like cutting the cords between you. Especially if they are very ill. This is extremely important otherwise the ill person will unknowingly continue to take from your energy supply and you will notice how drained you feel.

It is also advisable to reground yourself after you send healings to refuel your own energy tank. Either stand outside on grass or in your room and say " I ground myself to earth" and inhale the earth energy up through the feet visualizing strong roots. You only need to do this a few breaths.

**Note: Reiki is energy so the person you are sending it to does NOT need to be with you physically. If you don't know the person, asking for a photo beforehand may help you visualize the connection.

**NEVER send GR to anyone when you are tired. It will drain you. I know a few stories from others including myself, where we send healings while in bed either to our partner if they are unwell or to someone distantly and we forgot to disconnect and fell asleep. That is a big no-no and you will regret it because you'll likely feel drained all day the next day.

BENEFITS of 3 minute Gendo Reiki for Work

The challenges in a company environment. How to increase performance using reiki to create synergy in the team.

Even if you are enjoying the work field you are in, the time crunch and deadlines can still create an environment of issues such as stress, anxiety, isolation, depression, fatigue/sleep disorders, eating disorders and Professional burnout. If a company were to realign as a team through the Gendo Reiki and maintain a daily practice, they can commonly notice reduced stress, reduced anxiety, relief from burnout, improved professional relationships, enhanced awareness and improved strategic thinking. They will be able to manage their Gendo lines to be open to new approaches, changes and follow the trends of technology and the "new normal".

For adhering to the pre-Covid ways of doing business is no longer effective. There will be a lot of skepticism at meetings as people reconfigure and brainstorm. But there's a fine line between skepticism and stubbornness. When you see the signs and the evidence that change in business tactics is necessary but still remain skeptical, it may be more of a sign of indecisiveness rather than a healthy questioning mindset. You may miss opportunities if your boundaries are coming from resistance to change. So let's imagine a typical hectic schedule at work and see how you and your team can still hold the zen way of action if you develop a daily practice.

Problem-solution: 11 Steps to reduce stress at work

> *Einstein; "you can't solve a problem with the same mind that created it"*

1: Exhaustion- "Energy" 3 min GR meditation

2: Headache - Golden sunlight dispersing it 3 min GR meditation

3: Overtime - more tired, longer results, G e n d o line: Sleep and wake up early to finish.

4: Brain Fog - causes mistakes. leads to missed deadlines: GR for focus

5: Tension at meetings or w VIP clients - no agreement, discord leads to longer meetings, no results. Take a 5 minute timeout: Do a Group GR to regroup, refocus

6: Pain point: bills, stress, fear leads to tension, tight cluttered thoughts: GR for "Clarity, Peace": use Golden Sun Reiki

7: Important client call : needs to be clear, strong persuasive but if you speak in a dull, tired voice, a prospect will lose interest: Samurai Mudra GR to get grounded before the call

8: Doubts, skepticism: Hinders progress of decision-making: GR to "focus for right decisions".

9: Issues at home : ADD, Autistic child, college funds, mortgages. GR golden sun for Peace and calm

10: Fevers: absentee: GR for fever. It really works!!

11: No time to exercise: leads to Obesity, poor diets, more tension, vicious cycle. we NEED downtime to regenerate: GR for heart to open. self love, encourages you to change lifestyle.

NOTES

Chapter 7:

Developing a Samurai Gendo Lifestyle

"The more control you have, the more freedom you have, isn't it? Less control you have, more entanglement you have, less freedom" Sahdguru
Spiritual Leader

What can you do after you finish the attunements and you want to bring it into your world? What would be the physical process of this energy. Well, in order <u>to fully absorb the Gendo into your life, you must learn by doing</u>. Following the philosophy of practicing by doing is the best way to absorb it. It is to <u>get in touch with self-awareness of your actions</u>. You could read amazing recipes in a gourmet cookbook with delicious photos of the dishes all you want, even have the ingredients, but that knowledge won't help you become a top chef until you start practicing and truly appreciate the art of mastery.

When I reflect on my childhood, despite the drawbacks in my health, I have been blessed with caring parents and siblings and experienced three very distinct educations in three different cultures; United States, England and Japan. In a funny way it was almost a backwards kind of upbringing where I learned to be independent and outspoken in the US, then suddenly put into an all girls school in the Convent of Notre Dame run by nuns in London where I was trained to be a well behaved, polite little lady and finally moved back to Tokyo as a teenager with no clue on my original culture. My mother never tried to send us to a japanese school on weekends like all other Japanese parents were doing. However, over the years spent in Tokyo, learning to live in a more restricted, conservative environment, I began to appreciate the quiet beauty in their nature and art which contrasted to the lively and mellifluous chatter of their language. There is an innate quality of honor and respect that comes from deep within their DNA that appears in their way of living that comes naturally to them. It is this Zen lifestyle practice that I wanted to incorporate into my teachings through Gendo Reiki.

Here is a list of 16 Daily Habits to Condition Yourself to start developing Gendo and maintain the Reiki alignments.

1: The daily ritual of meditation: The 3 minute Gendo. To ground and set your focus for the day.

Absorbing the pyramid energy of Chichen Itza, New Mexico, January, 2020

2: How can you be of service today (vs. what's in it for me.)

3: Declutter routine: Start with making your bed. Washing dishes after every meal.

4: Nutrition : Choosing healthy, colorful food. Thanking the food

5: Physical activity. Posture: Slouching closes in your vibration. Walking: how we're going forward in the world. Good posture amplifies your energy field or aura.

6: Non-violent communication. Swearing and aggression hertz disrupts balance

7: Observe body language. Ex. crossed arms closes your vibration. Defensive Hertz

8: Using a short break to practice a 3 minute reiki on something: Ex. energy, refocus.

9: **Listen well** and practice reading people's vibrations (vibes)
   Being respectful. In your manners and words. Not to be pushy.

10: Allow others to be who they are and focus on how you could shift instead.
   Learn to catch yourself in a bad habit.

> *Detachment doesn't mean not caring.*
> *It's taking care of yourself first and letting others*
> *take responsibility for their actions Without trying to*
> *save or punish them.*

11: Being honest. Integrity. Genuine

12: Engaging another person. Sharing and connecting

13: Performing a random act of kindness. Magnifies your Heart

14: Being barefoot on grass, and indoors to feel connection to earth.

15: Saying thank you. Being thankful

16: Sleep. Restoring vibrational balance

There is a well known Monk trained in the Shaolin temples by the name of Master Shi Zheng Yi who talks about the 5 hindrances of Success:

1: Temptation

2: Negative emotions

3: Non-motivation, sleepiness

4: Restlessness which reflects an unsettled mind

5: A skeptical mind equals an indecisive mind

He said you need to align yourself and create structure in your life; create a plan to remove these obstacles. So don't let these hindrances get in your way to practice.

<u>NOTES</u>

CONCLUSION:

Ikigai "A reason for being"

Spirit without matter is motionless;matter without spirit is lifeless (arch mic youtube)

Another reason I developed this style of Energywork is because I saw the growing awareness and interest in minimalism and how a decluttered life does help lower stress. There was a study recently of measuring anxiety levels based on living in a very untidy room versus a simple, clean one showing a significant drop in stress after the space was decluttered. However, it's not easy for some to get the motivation to clear out the things that no longer serve them but I found that applying the healing energy of Gendo reiki augmented quite a few of my clients' desires to declutter their homes. It was an added bonus result I did not expect that helped them segue into the art of a zen lifestyle and honoring themselves, starting within their homes.

Another interesting Japanese expression that might help you imagine the results of Gendo Reiki is the term "Ikigai".

Ikigai 生き甲斐 (pronounced: "ikigai") is hard to

translate into one word but carries a depth into what one needs to feed one's spirit

Definition: A Japanese concept that means **"A reason for being".**

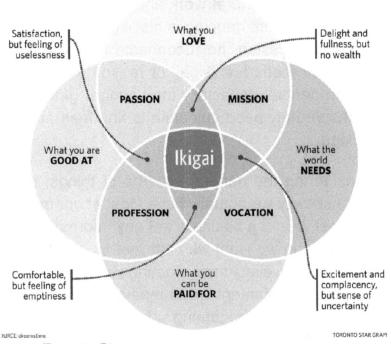

Ikigai
A JAPANESE CONCEPT MEANING "A REASON FOR BEING"

Satisfaction, but feeling of uselessness

What you **LOVE**

Delight and fullness, but no wealth

PASSION

MISSION

What you are **GOOD AT**

Ikigai

What the world **NEEDS**

PROFESSION

VOCATION

Comfortable, but feeling of emptiness

What you can be **PAID FOR**

Excitement and complacency, but sense of uncertainty

SOURCE: dreamstime

TORONTO STAR GRAPH

Image: Toronto Star

The word refers to having a direction or purpose in life which brings out your passion to engage in something that makes one's life worthwhile. It is when an individual takes spontaneous and willing actions towards accomplishing something, giving them satisfaction and a sense of meaning to life. It carries a nuance of satisfying one's spirit rather than the ego, almost like creating your successes while respecting and unifying all areas of your life around what gives you joy, without compromising anything. A great example is the Japanese movie "Shall we dance", in which the lead is a husband who reaches his Genkai, (reached past his limits), becoming spiritually empty in his canned routine at work and at home. He soon discovers ballroom dancing is his 'ikigai' and through his growing passion, he reconnects to his wife and child, which feeds his 'ikigai' or reason to be. Think of all the people, especially the younger generation, who desperately need guidance to find their purpose and 'ikigai'.

Considering the general scheme of things, in our modern society we actually have most of our material needs met. We can basically get any information and order anything we want with internet technology. We have schools on every topic meeting our mental needs. The vast entertainment world meets our appetite for fun.. Everything is becoming attainable at a click of a button. But what this social upheaval is perhaps teaching us all, is that none of the above is really what fulfills what I term true success and happiness. There is one more major area that makes us innately human and yet is so overlooked: Our spirit. We simply are not just a body and mind. Relying on the mind and body to navigate through life is going to end in disappointments if you don't connect to the vibration of your spirit. Intellect alone will not be enough to help you achieve true harmony and balance. There would always be a sense of emptiness.

As I write during this COVID time, I think isolation has truly made us realize how much we humans depend on human contact; to be physically present. Our spirits thrive through connecting and sharing. Lockdowns have shown us how profound this need is. To be seen. To be heard. The mark of true success is how to make a difference to others and they to us. People helping each other. You often hear from those who reached the top of fame and fortune that it's not all that it's cracked out to be. These types have lost their sense of Self to the public, Their Gendo lines are invaded and their acts have become meaningless to them.

Did you know that science now recognizes that trees communicate? They send vibrational frequencies through their roots and if one tree is not healthy, they are able to send it life force energy in the form of carbon. (Canadian ecologist researcher Suzanne Simard). Certain tree species also seem to recognize a foreign tree amongst their midst and divert the food source away from that unwelcome tree to weaken it. In other words, we too, as a community, can learn to recognize when someone or something needs help or repair and to also work as a team to dissolve, or reform vibrational threats to our well being such as fear induced propaganda.

People don't realize that instead of only using the mind and body to make things happen, it is much more effective to come from the frequency flow of your heart together with your brainwaves.'What's in it for me' is not as meaningful as 'How can I be of service?'. The former keeps you calculating and stagnant. The end profit is fleeting and even lonely. But if you approach life's opportunities from the heart to see how you and your skills could benefit and make a difference to others, the act and the reward amplifies your spirit which is the sum total of who you are. Isn't that success?

One of the permanent results I gained through Gendo Reiki was developing a natural ability to step back and observe. I can listen at a deeper level and tune in to situations. I read people better so I can make clearer decisions. I am able to adjust or adapt smoothly to whatever issues arise and I can see how I can help clients more efficiently. Of course I have my moments like anyone but my life feels much less complicated and it's easier to brush aside things that used to bother or worry me.

> *"When you talk, you are only repeating what you already know. But if you listen, you may learn something new"* Dalai Lama

The Gendo technique does not teach you more stuff to do but rather it shows you a different potential of yourself. When you are aligned, your vibration attracts the right people and information to you, showing you more clearly who you genuinely are. Have you ever sat under a freezing waterfall in cold weather? You have to act on the 5 second impulse because once you think about it.. the courage goes away. But when I am sitting under one, it's the most powerful experience. You need to be grounded or else the water will push you down.

There's no room to think about it, except to focus on being grounded. Then at a sudden point...there's no sound.. I become so very still inside, so peaceful. I feel my spirit. And when I step out.. everything looks crystal clear and colors are vibrant, I believe my vibration is in sync with all that is. The rest of the day I'm in a kind of silent trance. I feel so pure I don't want to ruin it by chatting.

I believe Gendo Reiki can be your waterfall. To cleanse and clear your spirit so you have a chance to redefine yourself. To attract the right vibration of other people that matches yours, to learn to repel situations that do not serve you, using your Gendo lines. To know how you can be of service.

TESTIMONIALS:

CLIENTS

"I have taken the Gendo Reiki with Lisa and have found the sessions and practice to be very beneficial in my workplace. I use it to keep myself and my patients calm. She is a powerful teacher."
Dr. P Saddler, MD. PHD.
MD. PHD.,N. Hospital, New York City

"I work overtime everyday in a highly aggressive environment. I'm always tense and exhausted. Using the tools of the Gendo help me to stay calm and to be prepared. My colleague and I took Lisa's courses and apply it before we start work."
Fadhil A
Correction Officer, High Security Facility, NJ

"My experience with Lisa has been amazing. She has improved my intuition and my ability to relate with others. My problem solving ability has soared. When students seek my advice, I seem to be able to help them in exactly the way that they need".
Marilyn Horowitz, Professor, NYU

"After Lisa's program, I feel very relaxed.
I felt the strong energy. It's very hectic at
work, so I practice the 3 minute meditation
to stay calm and keep the office calm"
Dr. Eliso. N
Doctor, NYC Hospital

"The Gendo Reiki course adds to your
ability to tap into the energy that flows
through you. I highly recommend these
sessions and working with Lisa".
Robert Manni
Reiki Master, Hypnotherapist

"To be honest, I was very skeptical, but I
felt the energy getting stronger after each
level. It was amazing feeling! It helps give
me energy to work and calms the negativity
at home too."
Kayo M
Massage Therapist

"I've practiced other modalities, but Lisa's
program really helped get rid of the "brain
fog". A year later and I still feel much
more in control and focused. She is very
powerful!"
Paula S
United Nations

"Lisa Okochi has worked with several of my

psychotherapy groups. My clients found her thoughtful, insightful and helpful, teaching them techniques to deal with their anxiety. I would highly recommend her."
Dr Joseph L.Ph.D.
Director of Postgraduate, Center of Psychotherapy, NYC

"Lisa Okochi is a gifted healer (and a nice person). Lisa's Gendo reiki course is a powerful healing technique that created profound and permanent shifts in my life. Namely, my issues with anger subsided. I also am attracting better relationships and work into my life. My relationship with my mother and difficult friendships turned around. Sending them healing reiki changed their interactions with me and I with them. On an unconscious level you need to be ready for these changes, but when you are, lisa, who comes from a lineage of healers, will be there to expertly guide you to a better place in your life. I have gone to many healers in the past and perhaps they did heal me, but Lisa's work created tangible shifts in my life. At times, it seems magical"
Deborah, Child development Specialist on early prevention, 5/2020

"It was lovely! I feel better than I have

in weeks. The pink moon was streaming through the window. I was yawning so much which for me is a sign of release of tension. And tears flowed too. It was a lovely experience. Amy also loves it. Thank you."
Adele College Professor and Educational Consultant, 5/2020

"Hands down if not the best session:I've ever had. I'm so high, so light feeling, my energy feels so grounded. I saw so many colors, and smokey colors, I could see a pin drop of your intention and the whole area just warmed and cooled. Lisa, thank you so SO so much, absolutely in awe!"
Shaun LMT 3/2020

"When my friend's heart condition became so weak that he needed surgery, I sent him Gold Gendo Reiki for a few minutes a few times a day from pre-op to post-op. He recovered at such a fast pace that the Drs even commented on it and my friend felt calm throughout when he usually gets very anxious. I know it was the reiki. It feels good to help in this way then just to sit and hold his hands. I feel I helped more."
Aleksandra, Entrepreneur 8/2019

"I was familiar with Reiki, but not with Gendo. At first, I was skeptical and intrigued at the same time, but I felt I needed to be "cleansed, have my mind reset" since I had been going through a lot of anxiety and some other personal issues at that time, so I figured why not try it. I was open to explore it further, however, did not really expect much from it. I was wrong is all I can say.

I decided to join a group class because I found it is a richer experience than going solo. Interacting directly with people in the same room, both the teacher and other students, enlivens the learning experience in many ways. At the first class, Lisa broke down the process in a logical, step-by-step way that made it all very easy to understand. She spoke in a way that everyone could assimilate, even people who had not had a background in any spiritual practice. The session was amazing! Then, several other sessions followed... I felt as if a ton of bricks were taken off my shoulders, felt at peace and was finally able to deal with so many unsolved issues.

But keep in mind that GR is not something that will give you superpowers. Like everything in life, it requires practice. It is not like you have an epiphany and then ... boom... everything is perfect. It can be transformative, but it is a gradual awakening from your preconceived mode of daydreaming.

I have to add that Lisa is very welcoming, non-judgmental, even-tempered, professional, and she has clear boundaries and communicates clearly.

Thanks to this, I am in a such a greater state of mind spiritually, emotionally and mentally. This really helped me to be more focus in life and be grounded again, showed me a way to live my life "happier" than before."
Verissimo, Wall Street, 12/2019

"I want to thank you for attuning me to GR, for your teachings, for giving me guidance of what I should pay attention to, to keep growing. This is important for me because growing spiritually, being connected and aligned to my true self is my priority. After all our sessions, I feel more awareness of myself, paying more attention to my feelings, knowing more about myself. Now I'm working on converting this knowledge to action to make it conscious and regular. I have more clarity about myself and my next steps thank you again!"
Eugene, Web Consultant, 6/2020

"I met Lisa by noticing a flyer posted in my building advertising her services which was for Reiki healing.. It took a while for me to contact Lisa because of my uncertainty, whether what I was experiencing could be helped with Reiki. The year was 2011. At the time, I was suffering from a deep depression after the death of my beloved husband, and I knew that I could not go on with what I was experiencing and feeling. I contacted Lisa and she helped me tremendously and after a few sessions I started feeling that the Reiki was healing me and after a few more sessions I could feel my transitioning from the darkness inside of me to feeling this bright white light energizing me, and when I got home I just knew that I was feeling like a new person, and can honestly say that to this day, I have never felt better. Thank you Lisa!!!".
Linda Education department

"Working with Lisa Okochi and her teachings of Gendo reiki has strengthened my connection with my higher-self and assisted me in removing my past judgmental self to approach situations from a more balanced center, a non-duality point-of-view. While going through each level, my friends, co-workers immediately began

to notice a new brightness in my face and a slightly softer pitch in my voice tone. In my career, I help people on a daily basis and I've noticed since working with Lisa my conversations with clients have become deeper which has helped me find a stronger solution to their problems and needs."
Alex S, Publicist, Producer. Nov 2020

"When I first started GR. I was in a dark place grieving the loss of my sister. I was hopeless and defeated. I remember the first session all I could do was cry. And when I was taught to cut the cords it was life changing. I started the healing process. I was able to re-invent my business and ensure I set boundaries between my staff and clients I served. I used it to help the babies I treated to stop crying and begin to heal the pain and discomfort they were feeling but couldn't express. My family and I started shifting. We argued less and loved more. My husband was calm and my daughter was in such good spirits. The physical pain I felt in my knees that almost crippled me some days improved drastically. My manifestation started to emerge right before my eyes. GR has truly helped improve my family and work life. As well as overall health and self healing.

I shall forever be grateful to the support and assistance Lisa provided me. I am truly thankful from the bottom of my heart. May your dreams and wishes come true right before your eyes. Thanks again. It had been life changing your a natural healer."
Jessica F, Daycare owner
Nov 2020

Alex S, Publicist, Producer.
Nov 2020

PET TESTIMONIALS FROM OWNERS

"I contacted Lisa to help our sick cat, Mamma who was listless, with chronic headaches and IBS and after 2 short, mini healings done remotely, she was looking much calmer, more playful and still maintaining better digestion 5 weeks later. She's done a total 180! Lisa even said things about our cat she couldn't possibly know. Like an animal communicator...She also has helped me a lot in recent years with her Energy Work."

Catherine, College student Consultant, 5/2020

"My dog Layla was only 5 weeks old when it got very sick and we all thought she was going to leave us when Lisa sent Reiki to her distantly. We didn't tell her what was wrong but she said she felt Layla vomiting and having seizures, which was true! We noticed our puppy getting better after the healing and now she's a healthy 2 year old. Thank you Lisa!"
Julia, Entrepreneur, 6/2020

"My last dog Poochy, at 16 yo, after 2 operations of removal of tumors in her belly, had a problem with walking again. I always had to lift her up in order to move or walk. Last she walked assisted by me and she collapsed and couldn't get up again. I invoked the Gendo Reiki I had just learned that day to help her get up. After a few moments she got up by herself and walked towards the door where she collapsed again.

I had to take her to the Animal Hospital in Yonkers where she was put to sleep. But was grateful to see her walk one last time. I have since been practicing it everyday for my family and keep in touch with Lisa."
Freda 9/2017-2020

"I wanted to go away for a few days but my four cats were behaving aggressively towards one another for some reason and I didn't feel confident to hire a cat sitter but when I told Lisa the situation, she said I should do the reiki on them as a group to get along in peace. So I did a few minutes once or twice a day not sure if I was doing it right. Well after a couple of days I actually could see they had stopped hissing and were quietly together. I was able to go away with peace of mind".
TR. Graphic designer 8/2020

BIBLIOGRAPHY:

"Mind to matter": Dawson Church

"Emotional Wisdom": Dena Saxer and Mantak Chia"

"The Unfettered Mind": Takyan Soho" The Art of War" Sun Tsu: James Clavell "Hagakure": Yamamoto Tsunemoto

"The Book of Five Rings" : Miyamoto Mushashih "Focus": Eugene Gendlin

" The seven habits of highly effective people":

Stephen R. Covey "Boundaries": Dr Henry Cloud

"The Bhagavad-Gita": Barbara Stoler Miller "Simple Qi Gong": Mantak Chia

"The Road Less Travelled" : M. Scott Peck M.D

https://nextshark.com/samurai-women-history-forgo t/

Japan times on female samurai https://www. japantimes.co.jp/life/2011/10/09/general/women-warriors-of-japan/#.Xfm1HK5OmaO

https://www.myhighplains.com/news/for-your-
health/research-shows-burning-sage-kills-94-
of-airborne- bacteria/

Kundalini Reiki. Ole Gabrielsen

AUTHOR BIO

I am from a lineage of healers on my mother's side and Samurai dating back to 700 A.D. on my paternal side. I became aware of the world of healing from a young age and discovered what true empowerment means. My journey began, chanting with monks and sitting under waterfalls, studying healing modalities, honing my skills.  Going deep into Ashtanga Yoga in Japan, I began to observe and develop the inner stillness of Zen being and grounding in the stance of my Samurai ancestors.

I love humanity and want to ease the suffering by clearing emotional blockages so they can see their true potential, learn to know their boundaries and become stronger in calmness. A graduate of ICU in Intercultural Communications, I am presently in New York, a Wellness/Spiritual Coach, Yoga instructor and Founder of Gendo Reiki; training and healing clients internationally.

Printed in the USA
CPSIA information can be obtained
at www.ICGtesting.com
LVHW080054091123
763364LV00005B/53